CW00797315

Breaking Through the Mist

Breaking Through the Mist

In Search of
the Meaning of Life

Thomas Burns

ANTIPOLIS PRESS
LIVINGSTON, MONTANA

To Charlene

Breaking Through the Mist
In Search of the Meaning of Life

Text, photos, and design by Thomas Burns

ISBN: 979-8-218-35453-4

Printed in Korea
Limited Edition of 500

Antipolis Press
501 S. 7th St., Livingston, Montana 59047
406-220-3905
thomasburns333@gmail.com

Where there is nothing, there is God.

William Butler Yeats

Contents

Introduction   Imagine   viii

Chapter One   Know Yourself   1

Chapter Two   To Be Loved   27

Chapter Three   Finding Happiness   47

Chapter Four   The Secret to Life   73

Chapter Five   The Eternal Portal   99

Chapter Six   Your Purpose on Earth   129

Chapter Seven   Change the World   155

Chapter Eight   Be Nothing   185

Chapter Nine   Be a Dreamer   203

Imagine

Imagine being transported to the past, peering into the future, or having many of life's most profound questions answered to your full satisfaction. Imagine knowing when to pull back, push ahead, or make critical decisions with total confidence. Wouldn't having these grand abilities constitute the grail humanity has been seeking since time immemorial?

Some might admonish you for delving into areas they believe should be left to the theologians, or question why you need to know more than what's been penned in the world's sacred texts. But given the opportunity, many would give up everything to access such wisdom.

Breaking Through the Mist, In Search of the Meaning of Life, is a compilation of knowledge and wisdom drawn from the higher collective consciousness—the vibratory realm of spirit where life's grander thoughts and concepts exist, the *Akashic* dimension where every break-through in planetary evolution originates.

In my search for the meaning of life I've discovered that the treasures of the higher realms are accessible to anyone through meditation, intuition, dreams, creativity, or any modality that connects one directly to their higher self—with this caveat: You must first crack the code of your eternal soul *on your own terms.*

My passion in life is to give voice to spirit through words and images. My creative process gives me access to the inner workings of physical reality, where the gears and pulleys operate behind the scenes of life. Through meditation, study, journaling, and trial and error, I've developed a personal Rosetta Stone that allows me to interpret the causal world around me.

Taking the creative path requires an open and inquisitive mind. In the course of my search for life's answers, I've undergone a dramatic shift in consciousness from that of my early upbringing and social conditioning. How I perceive myself, others, life, death, and the world in general evolved in ways I could never have imagined in my youth. However, what I learned and witnessed firsthand did not occur in a vacuum.

My quest began in earnest after having had an out-of-body experience while journaling in a coffee shop in Livingston, Montana. Initially, I struggled to make sense of what happened. But over time, having read similar accounts of others, I realized there's more to physical reality than what we perceive through our five senses.

Throughout my life, pivotal events foreshadowed the person I'm becoming, usually occurring after having experienced a major loss, or having overcome some stubborn emotional or mental block. With each new change in consciousness a layer of mist shrouding my higher self lifted, revealing an enlightened way forward, a broader perspective, or, in rare instances, what I believe to be a vision of an etheric realm.

Did I accept everything I experienced at face value? *No.* Did my ego ever stop negating what my higher self insisted was true? Hardly. Whatever I don't understand I place on a mental shelf until such time an answer reveals itself.

My commitment in life is to accept myself as a multi-dimensional being, give form to the formless, plumb the depths of my heart, mind, and soul, and document my experiences as any writer or artist would. Applying the creative process to attain higher states of consciousness motivates me to roll out of bed every morning and embrace the full expression of my life.

Hopefully, reading *Breaking Through the Mist* will inspire you to begin or continue your own journey on the path of self-realization. As I've learned over the years, there's nothing more exhilarating than discovering who you are in spirit, and the higher purpose of your life.

Chapter 1

Know Yourself

3   Life's Ultimate Challenge

5   Who Are You?

6   How You See Yourself

9   You Are Unique

10   The Essential Question

12   Searching for Answers

15   A Front Row Seat

17   Make Peace With Yourself

19   Life Viewed from Outer Space

21   Wings of Acceptance

23   Why Question Life?

25   Kudos

Life's Ultimate Challenge

Your soul is a unique facet
of the universal mind,
existing simultaneously
on infinite planes of consciousness.
The essence of who you are
permeates every particle of light
that gives form and substance
to the all-intelligent universe.
Impressive as that sounds,
it doesn't lessen the difficulty
of knowing who you are
or the direction of your life.
Despite every scientific advancement
of our modern age,
to "know yourself" remains
life's ultimate challenge.

Who Are You?

Do you think of yourself as a physician,

teacher, author, athlete, or actress?

From a cosmic perspective, such titles

define one dimension of yourself.

We are not just our job descriptions,

but embodied spiritual beings

striving to expand our consciousness

through self-reflection, meditation,

life's experiences, and service to others.

Yet many attempt to elevate themselves

by their degrees, titles, or positions.

Some use status to control others

or to fill an emotional void.

The mystics say, only the love you've imparted,

the humility you've displayed,

and the wisdom you've earned,

ultimately define the person you are.

How You See Yourself

Many will judge you through the eyes

of their unresolved psychology,

but do they really know how far you've come?

You hope the world has taken note

of all the good things you've done—

but don't be naive. There are those

who see only your flaws and weaknesses.

But if you're striving to do your best,

why be concerned how others perceive you?

Who has a right to judge you, anyway?

No one's perfect. Everyone's winging it.

Consider those you love

and everything you've overcome in life.

What counts in the eternal sense

is how satisfied you are being you.

You Are Unique

Your higher self conspires with the universe

to awaken you from your cosmic sleep.

Prior to conception, a configuration of stars

aligned to set in motion the time, place,

genetic set of parents, and karmic circumstances

required for you to embody on earth.

Given your past spiritual attainment

and the wisdom you must still acquire,

your family and the landscape of your childhood

provided you the perfect opportunity

to know yourself in greater depth,

and to further develop patience with others.

The Essential Question

Most are too busy working or raising a family to consider whether

life has any deeper meaning, so they rely on the poets and philosophers.

Granted, family, friends, career, and a thousand other responsibilities

can sidetrack anyone from trying to make sense of life or the world.

But haven't there been times when you stood awestruck beneath

a canopy of stars at night and pondered your existence in the universe?

Or times you teetered on the brink of despair and found yourself

standing on the shore shouting to the wind, "What's my purpose in life?"

Searching for Answers

Metaphysicians believe that,

because of our unique frequencies of consciousness,

every person and circumstance in our lives

exists because of the law of attraction.

Mystics contend that we are born

to balance our karmic scales and to fulfill

a destiny that corresponds to our inner mastery

and continuing quest for enlightenment.

Yet there are those who insist

we have little or no control over our lives—

that we're at the complete mercy

of a random and unforgiving universe.

Such beliefs aside, at the deepest level of our souls,

aren't we all searching for ways

to enhance our happiness, expand our horizons,

and give flight to our dreams?

A Front Row Seat

Taking on a challenge bigger than ourselves,

guaranteed to test our mettle,

secures a front row seat

to the inner workings of the creative universe.

Whether caring for an aging parent,

opening your door to an unwanted child,

or providing hospice care for a stranger,

when engaged in the day-to-day drama

of tending to the needs of others,

your patience and resolve will be tested.

Granted, opening your heart to others

makes you an easy target in the world.

You set yourself up for rejection,

and you'll question your sanity at times.

But just before falling asleep at night,

you'll also know the tenacity of your spirit.

Make Peace With Yourself

Winter is the least cluttered season of the year

to resolve unfinished business—

a time to be honest with ourselves,

and take account of what's important in our lives.

A time to let go of old resentments,

and summon to the fore all that's been unsaid.

As winter draws closer to the bone,

simple gestures hold greater weight.

Perhaps a broken promise needs revisiting,

or a misunderstanding begs a letter.

Because thoughts and feelings reach

hearts and minds more directly during winter,

what whiter page of the year to make

lasting peace with ourselves and others?

Life Viewed from Outer Space

Every forest blanketing the earth

has its share of less-than-perfect trees—

especially those with contorted branches

straining mightily to reach the sun.

Yet every forest viewed from outer space

glistens like an emerald-colored sea.

Life is filled with loss and disappointments,

messy relationships, and unrealized dreams.

Yet our perpetually expanding consciousness

spirals beautifully and rhythmically

toward the source of our eternal existence.

We all have our share of imperfections—

some in plain sight, others deeply hidden.

But like the forest viewed from outer space,

we all glisten like an emerald sea.

Wings of Acceptance

Accepting who you are

despite what others think or say

means embracing everything

that makes you *you*—flaws and all.

It means accepting your strengths

and weaknesses alike,

for they surely balance one another out

to make you whole.

Given human evolution,

we're all destined to defy gravity and fly.

At each metamorphic stage

we can appear gangly at times.

But those who love themselves,

even as 16-legged caterpillars,

believe that every stage of evolution

is beautiful.

Why Question Life?

Many skate along the surface of their lives

oblivious to their purpose or potential.

They rarely question whether life has any deeper meaning

other than to live and die.

Yet scientists have found a link between the time

humans first began to question life's purpose

and every consequential breakthrough

in planetary evolution.

Poets have long mused that life is that much richer

when its deeper meanings are contemplated.

Philosophers contend that, by pondering

life's existential possibilities, we discover

hidden dimensions of ourselves

that enhance love, happiness, and creativity.

And the mystics?

Asked whether life has any greater purpose,

they only smile.

Kudos

Given the challenges you overcame

throughout this and past lifetimes,

you would be amazed to see the progress

of your soul in that arc of time.

When the weight of life came crashing down,

testing you unmercifully,

you kept the fires of hope and optimism

burning brightly on your altar.

The lessons that you spun to gold

earned you a coveted position

in the hierarchy of souls who guide humanity

through the evolutionary maze.

Having awakened to your soul's needs,

and the needs of others in the world,

those further up the mountain

applaud your constancy of spirit.

Chapter 2

To Be Loved

29   Being Real

30   Someone, Somewhere

33   For Love to Be Returned

35   A Currency Earned

37   Petals of Ourselves

39   Live for Love

41   Portrait of Yourself

43   Mend a Broken Heart

45   The Dream of Life

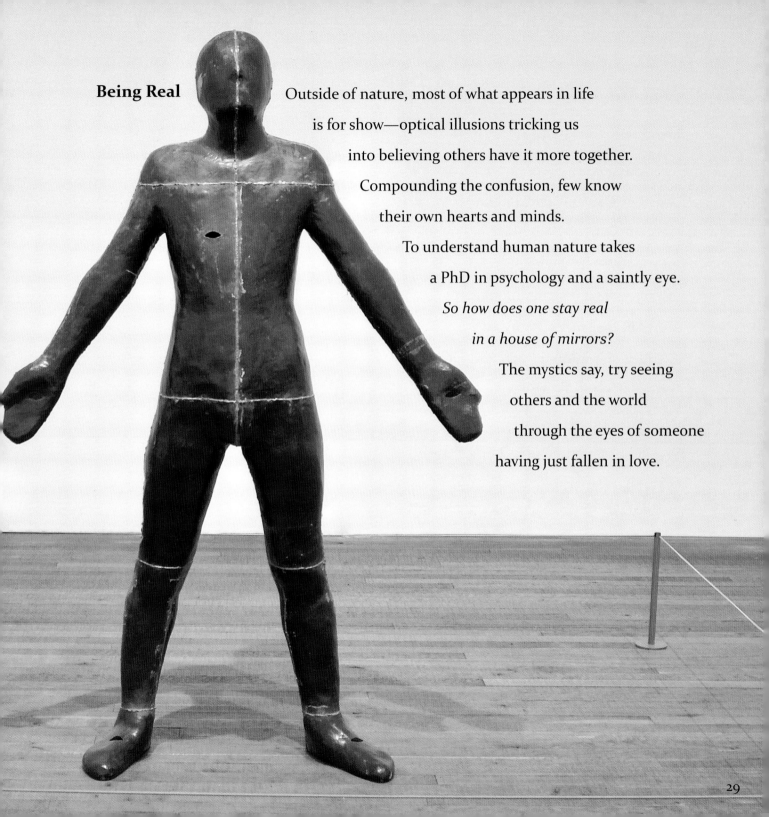

Being Real

Outside of nature, most of what appears in life
is for show—optical illusions tricking us
into believing others have it more together.
Compounding the confusion, few know
their own hearts and minds.
To understand human nature takes
a PhD in psychology and a saintly eye.
So how does one stay real
in a house of mirrors?
The mystics say, try seeing
others and the world
through the eyes of someone
having just fallen in love.

Someone, Somewhere

There's always someone, somewhere,

who complements your heart and mind.

But you must set the stage,

for love is drawn to safe and warm encounters.

To attract that special someone,

you must do something extraordinary.

Arrange the stars to spell your name out brightly

across the midnight sky.

Stretch beneath the sun and offer God

everything you own, and then some.

Let the white sand beach beneath your feet

guide you to the cove of dreams.

Having set the alchemy, that special someone

who complements your heart and mind

is bound by laws of love to seek you out

because your name is written in the stars.

For Love to Be Returned

Despite their struggles,

and what their parents taught them,

those who raised you likely did their best

given what they knew.

By example, right or wrong,

you learned to be self-sufficient,

especially when it came to matters

relating to the heart.

But parents are not perfect.

Being human, they have blinders.

Maybe you were taught that money,

fame, position, or beauty attracts love,

only to discover later that,

having been rejected by another,

you must be honest with yourself first

for love to be returned.

A Currency Earned

Demanding love from others
only pushes them away.
No one takes pleasure being saddled
by another's expectations.
Those demanding love,
believing they're entitled,
lose sleep at night if no one writes
or returns their calls.
Love cannot be forced.
It must be given freely
without demands or expectations.
Ask any happy couple
who've been together fifty years.
Love's a currency that's earned,
not a debt to be collected.
When circulated freely,
love returns a thousandfold.

Petals of Ourselves

How do you explain falling in love
to those still searching?
Millions of words have been penned
to express the sentiment,
but words fall to their knees
in the brightness of love's light.
Love is different to the young
than to those about to die,
or to a newly committed couple
embraced in one another's arms.
Love can be expressed many ways,
but when given freely,
it strips away our fragile pretense,
exposing who we truly are.
What we share with others
is the fallen petals of ourselves.

Live for Love

The all-pervading force of the universe

that keeps the world from falling into chaos,

let's call LOVE—the super glue

that keeps everything sanely together.

Look into the cosmic mirror and describe

all your loving and redeeming qualities.

Be honest, use your imagination—

for love is infinitely textured and nuanced.

Loving yourself and others

is the boldest path anyone can take.

On your final breath, you'll clearly see

how love weaved its way throughout your life.

Hasn't everything you've said and done

revolved around giving or receiving love?

When loving yourself and others,

you make the world a saner place for everyone.

Portrait of Yourself

The primary job of the ego

is to protect us from pain and disappointment.

On clear and sunny days, it reminds us

that thunderstorms are in the forecast.

When starting something new,

it calculates why we might not succeed.

To offset the pangs of losing,

it lowers our expectations of winning.

But just as our ego protects us

from the pain and disappointments of life,

it can also stifle our success

by keeping us from dreaming big.

To keep its voice from droning in your head,

be like the artist who envisions

the portrait of himself as a finished masterpiece,

even before he sets up his easel.

By seeing yourself as a work-in-progress,

the ego has nothing left to complain about.

Mend a Broken Heart

To mend a broken heart,

try this alchemical technique—

a little-known secret the mystics say

can change your life forever.

On a blank sheet of paper,

list all your struggles and regrets.

Separately, list everything

and everyone you're grateful for.

In a ritual of self-forgiveness,

burn your list of old regrets,

then place what you're grateful for

by your bedside to be read nightly.

Affirming what's positive in life,

and letting go of what isn't,

opens the floodgates of love

to fill any empty heart.

The Dream of Life

Those living in the cosmic flow

say the magic of life's journey

holds greater pleasure than

any momentary thrill of arriving.

The sage is grateful for whatever pillow

he rests his head upon.

He believes his needs are met

even before they physically appear.

He accepts everyone unconditionally—

rich, poor, high, and low.

Acts of kindness clear his head

and give his heart a steady beat.

And just as everything in the universe

has its own rhyme and purpose,

when living in the cosmic flow,

life streams magical in every moment.

Chapter 3

Finding Happiness

49   Everything in Stride

51   Letting Go

53   Make Life Easy

54   Your Life is Your Own

56   You're Rich

59   Old Souls

61   Happy People

62   When in Their Presence

65   The Price of Happiness

67   A Contented Life

69   Light of Wing

70   The Book of Happiness

Everything in Stride

The biggest challenge for most,

including spiritual masters, is being unaffected

by life's ever-changing circumstances.

Every moment is constantly in flux.

One minute you're relaxing on a sunny terrace

engrossed in a mesmerizing book,

a minute later you're scrambling for shelter

from an unexpected thundershower.

Your response to sudden storms reveals

your capacity to make the best of any situation.

Those who take their lives in stride

attract greater opportunities for happiness.

Perhaps while taking shelter,

the one you've been searching for all of your life

enters the room and sits down beside you.

Letting Go

Leverage the tides, time, and gravity

to work in your favor.

By your guidance, allow your children

to find their own way in life.

You can't control the wind

or a pack of wild wolves

any more than you can keep

two destined lovers apart.

When life becomes unbearable,

spill your guts out in a journal.

Letting go of what you can't control,

angels fill the void.

Inhale the day, exhale the night.

Let your dreams take their natural course.

Let each moment be your guide.

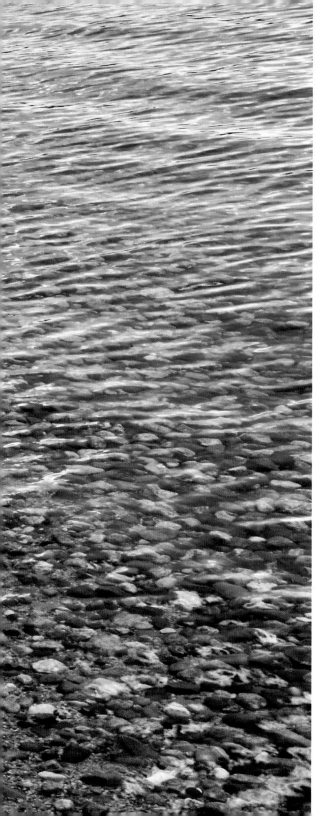

Make Life Easy

Some possess this uncanny awareness

that something profound

is percolating in and around them

that elevates their thinking

and sharpens their senses.

They say this feeling originates

from their unshakable belief

that life is easier than what they were taught,

and that too much time is wasted worrying.

Such souls live in the moment,

have long and loving relationships,

and are usually found on mountaintops

overlooking life's grander views.

And all they must do in return

to maintain their good fortune

is to ebb and flow with the tide of life.

Your Life is Your Own

Ultimately, no person, possession,

or adoring public can make you happy.

Happiness originates within.

Yet many in the world chase happiness

outside themselves through wealth,

status, or by their associations with others.

Life will never feel complete

until you mount your steed and ride out

to embrace the early morning sun.

Only then, by having made your life your own,

will happiness take the reins.

You're Rich

Maybe you're asking yourself why

you feel stuck in the back of the plane, squeezed

in the middle seat, while those in first class

enjoy better service and more legroom?

Or why you're spending more time than ever

scraping by financially, while others

appear to do little more than fly to exotic resorts

and dine at five-star restaurants?

Actually, entertaining such complaints is silly

to those living in third world countries.

From where they sit, you're rich!

They would gladly change seats with you any day.

Given that your life is seen as ideal

by the majority of the world, why complain?

Isn't life being content in the seat you're assigned,

whether it's first class or coach?

Old Souls

Old souls intuitively know
how to navigate life's complicated maze.
They're the first to offer a helping hand
or a listening ear to those in need.
They'll diffuse an argument
with a disarming smile, find common ground
with those they disagree with,
and hold everyone under the same soft light.
Old souls accept life's losses,
even when they seem unfair.
And though some have taken a few wrong turns,
they've learned from their mistakes.
Old souls are the trusty engines of the world,
pushing humanity forward
around the bend and up the mountain
for the clearest view of the stars.

Happy People

Have you ever wondered why
some people seem happier than others?
Psychologists have discovered
that happy people tend to pursue a passion
that not only inspires *them*,
but energizes love in the world.
Despite any personal challenges,
happy people are optimistic at the core,
living as if heaven had granted them
a second chance to get things right.
What sets happy people apart
from those still struggling
is their willingness to enter the fray of life
and assume whatever challenging role
they were destined to play.

When in Their Presence

Just as everyone walking the earth

is on a personal evolutionary journey,

happy people are quick to celebrate

how far each soul has traveled.

Because everyone has a worthy story to impart,

happy people lean forward in their chairs

to listen to what everyone has to say.

Because we're all integral

to the whole and harmony of humanity,

happy people advance their own soul's journey

by assisting those who've lost their way.

The reason we feel so comfortable

when standing in their presence

is that happy people focus only on the light

streaming from our hearts.

The Price of Happiness

To enhance your happiness,

make a list of all your needs and dreams.

Then write out in detail everything

you plan to offer God in return.

What!? Offer God?

Yes! Did you think happiness

falls freely from the sky?

It's found in beads of sweat and tears shed

striving to achieve your lofty goals.

And since happiness demands living freely,

anchor to the bedrock of your soul a promise

to do whatever happiness demands,

go wherever happiness leads you.

A Contented Life

Living a contented life
is fairly straightforward to most:
Strive to be at peace with yourself,
others, and the world;
embody the wisdom
brought down from the sacred mountain;
give freely of yourself to family,
friends, and the wider community;
pursue a lifelong passion
that inspires your soul to greater heights;
relinquish guilt, regret, and judgment;
and face death with a clear conscience.
More importantly,
live as if experiencing the beauty,
wonder, and magic of life
through the eyes of a curious child.

Light of Wing

Living the abundant life means

something different to everyone.

Some believe owning a columned mansion

or driving a red Porsche makes them rich.

Others say loving relationships

and vibrant health constitute wealth.

Though possessions enrich our lives,

if forced to choose, most would give up

everything they own to live another day.

Then there are those who believe

the abundant life is living freely—

the reason monks, seasoned travelers,

and the young possess or carry less.

Being light of wing, they say,

gives them flight to anywhere, anytime.

The Book of Happiness

As the author of your life, you can do anything,

live anywhere, become anyone.

Deep within your consciousness exists

a temple of light housing all your dreams—

those of having access to eternal wisdom,

creating a more compassionate world,

or walking the cobblestone streets of Paris

in conversation with someone you love.

On the central altar of your temple,

your personal book of happiness is found.

Turning the pages, recalling the joys

and struggles of your journey, you realize,

as the main character of your story,

you did your best to overcome life's challenges.

Given your wisdom and determination,

you authored a magical life for yourself

on the ever-winding road to happiness.

Chapter 4

The Secret to Life

75   Anything is Possible

77   The Secret to Life

79   You Have the Same Potential

80   Prosperity

83   Give of Yourself

85   When Losing Ground

86   Power of Gratitude

89   Surrender to the Universe

90   A Cosmic Game

93   Two Views of Life

94   The Creative Force

97   Welcome to Akasha

Anything is Possible

Though you were born on earth to revel

in its beauty, expand your wisdom and happiness,

and master time and space, you embodied

primarily to balance your karmic scales.

To that end, ask yourself whether

there are any traumatic events in your past

keeping you from living fully in the present?

Because healing begins on spiritual levels,

by extracting new insight from old traumas,

forgiving yourself and those involved,

and applying that newfound wisdom

to guide your life today,

you change your future for the better.

Your inner critic might scoff and argue:

The past is past and can never be changed.

But your inner mystic would likely counter:

In spiritual realms, anything is possible.

The Secret to Life

Most would agree

that life-changing events

often occur without warning,

or that a lifelong passion

can be sparked by a wild idea.

Could the secret to life

reveal itself just as easily?

You needn't join

an Eastern sect, or walk

the Way of the Cross—

the secret is found within.

For some, it's revealed

after having spent years

in prayer and discipline.

For others, it arrives

by simply holding

the hand of another.

You Have the Same Potential

How did Lao Tzu, the Buddha,
Plato, Pythagoras, Aristotle, Jesus,
Rumi, Gutenberg, Da Vinci,
Michelangelo, Magellan, Galileo,
Newton, Shakespeare, Franklin,
Jefferson, Mozart, Beethoven,
Lincoln, Austen, Darwin, Pasteur,
Edison, Tesla, Carver, Curie, Anthony,
Gandhi, Einstein, Turing, Hawking,
King, Mandela, and the Dalai Lama
help enlighten the world?
Each articulated a grander vision
of how our lives could be,
and by their genius, propelled humanity
to greater heights.

Prosperity

True prosperity is fired in the mind,

forged on the anvil of creativity,

tempered by unwavering belief,

and multiplied by loud outbursts of gratitude.

While many believe that prosperity

is measured by the things they own,

to the sage, it's the freedom of being detached

from the material world.

Prosperity originates in the belief

that we're all worthy of life's bounty.

But that belief must be as strong as a river

rushing wildly to the sea.

Those who believe that prosperity

is happiness, health, and wisdom,

and changing the world for the better,

are further ahead than most.

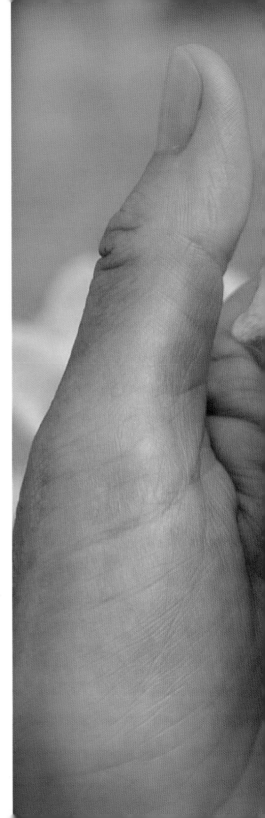

Give of Yourself

To bolster a flagging relationship, fulfill a lifelong dream,

or to encounter the love of your life, offer the universe something

of equal or greater value than your desire.

Heaven bends over backwards to provide your basic needs,

but if you require more, you must give more in return.

Hoping for a miracle cure or a lifelong partner without offering

the universe something big in return is just bad business.

Consider giving up smoking, complaining, or speaking ill of others.

To heal your body, pay the bills, or break a family spell,

plant the seeds of your desire deep within your consciousness.

While patiently waiting for those seeds to take root,

do good, meditate, pray, cut back, and return what you took in life.

Like any business, the universe expects a return on its investments.

Specifically, for you to start balancing your karmic ledger.

When Losing Ground

If spinning out of control, *let go*—

you have everything to gain.

Friendships, goals, and dreams

need fresh air and sunlight to grow.

Pressuring life to go one way

often creates the opposite effect.

Perhaps weeding your garden

or fly fishing on a picturesque river

is a better use of your time.

Writers gain fresh perspective

taking walks between drafts.

Relationships are strengthened

given healthy space apart.

Having lost your creative spark,

letting go allows the universe

to scan its entire network for inspiration

you may have overlooked.

Power of Gratitude

Expressing gratitude for every person,

circumstance, and possession in your life

stokes the eternal fires of creation—

the source of all your needs and dreams.

Being grateful for what you have and don't have

allows the universe to strengthen

the life force coursing through you.

Gratitude shields you from life's sticks and stones,

clears your head of dark clouds,

and accelerates physical healing.

Expressing gratitude attracts those to your life

willing to help advance your soul.

You begin to understand the purpose of others

and the cause of your struggles.

When grateful, whether standing in front

or at the back of a line,

you're content at either end.

Surrender to the Universe

You have the same potential as any sage
to be joyful, loved, and prosperous.
The practical sage fulfills his desires
by igniting his selfless intentions
on the front burners of his creative mind,
where spirit and matter burn hottest.
Believing his needs already met,
he releases any doubt to a higher power.
In response, the universe sets in motion
the most advantageous circumstances,
willing individuals, and the perfect time
required to fulfill all his needs.
Placing absolute trust in cosmic law,
he then goes about his usual business
with a knowing gleam in his eyes.

A Cosmic Game

Your higher self guides your life.

In the pursuit of happiness,

it orchestrates all your best moves.

When backed into a corner

or about to lose your edge,

your higher self calculates

the most effective means of escape.

To summon your spiritual guides

or to speak to God directly,

your higher self acts as emissary.

On the chessboard of life,

it plays a multi-dimensional game

with your lower self to keep you

several moves ahead.

Two Views of Life

Man has pondered

the purpose of life

since he first sought solace

in the constellations above.

Though less mystified today

than in centuries past,

many of life's contradictions

continue to perplex him.

Some will argue

we have only one life to live,

and that after death

we enter heaven, hell, or oblivion.

Others believe we evolve

over many lifetimes,

and that the ultimate goal of life

is oneness with all.

The Creative Force

Every thought, atom, and solar system

is held together by the creative force of the universe.

Our souls and the force are intrinsically one.

Anything is possible when wielding its power.

In eternal reality, there are no beginnings or endings;

no time between cause and effect;

no distance between planets and suns;

no line between past, present, and future.

Everything is interconnected. All is one.

The creative force connects you and me,

night and day, earth and sky, spirit and matter.

We are the brush, palette, canvas, and hand

of the creative force fulfilling our dreams.

Life's only restrictions are those we believe exist.

Welcome to *Akasha*

At a critical juncture in life, you might experience

a major breakthrough in consciousness,

when you're whisked to a realm outside of time—

one that mirrors your spiritual vibration, revealing

your purpose on earth, and what you must do

to rise to the next level of your soul's evolution.

Many achieve this heightened state through

meditation, determination, intense devotion,

or when having a near-death experience.

Welcome to the causal dimension of *Akasha!*

Upon arrival, you'll be given a tour behind the scenes

of your life for insight into what you must do

to further expand your heart and mind.

But know that, on returning to your everyday life,

your perception of reality will never be the same.

Chapter 5

The Eternal Portal

100	Open Your Mind
103	Two Paths Up the Mountain
104	Face to Face
107	Heaven on Earth
109	Between Two Rocks
110	Prepare for Adventure
112	Take the Leap
115	The Eternal Moment
117	A Lively Destination
118	The Hero's Quest
121	Causal Realms
123	Heaven Opens
125	Message of the Immortals
127	The Higher Dimensions

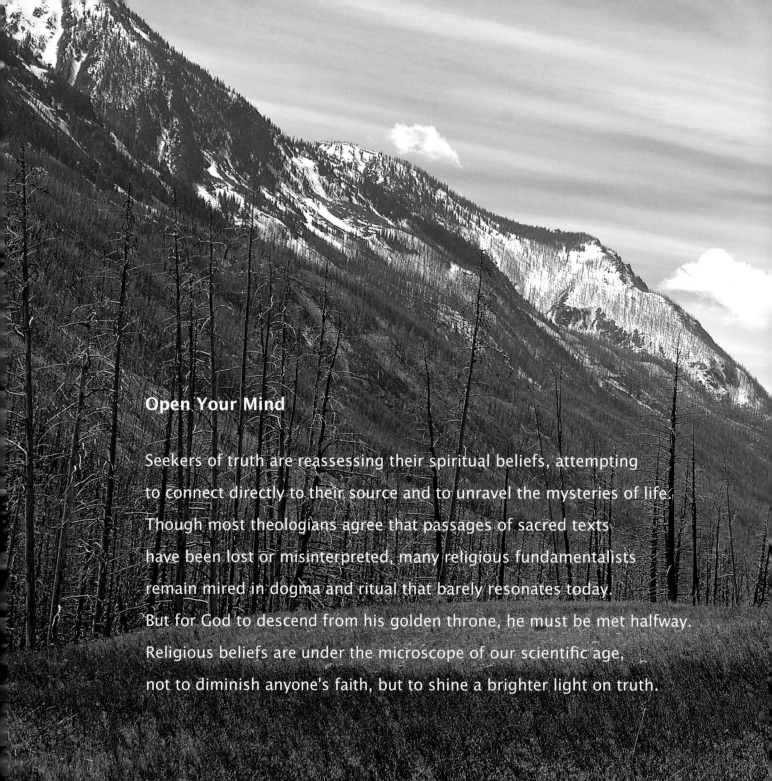

Open Your Mind

Seekers of truth are reassessing their spiritual beliefs, attempting

to connect directly to their source and to unravel the mysteries of life.

Though most theologians agree that passages of sacred texts

have been lost or misinterpreted, many religious fundamentalists

remain mired in dogma and ritual that barely resonates today.

But for God to descend from his golden throne, he must be met halfway.

Religious beliefs are under the microscope of our scientific age,

not to diminish anyone's faith, but to shine a brighter light on truth.

Two Paths Up the Mountain

Spiritual beliefs span the entire spectrum

of human consciousness.

Some believe God is a fire and brimstone deity;

that their religion is the one true faith;

that one must die in order to enter heaven;

that divine revelation ended with the old prophets;

that only the ordained priests

are privy to the secrets of redemption;

or that, by invoking the name of Jesus or Allah,

one's transgressions are absolved

without any karmic consequences.

Then there are those who believe

that God is found atop a mountain

of love and kindness.

Face to Face

There are major events in life
that force us to awaken quickly.
Times when we must summon
all our emotional stamina to the fore.
Maybe it's cancer, a breakup,
or the death of a loved one—
traumatic events that trigger
a reassessment of who we are,
and what's important in our lives.
Times that force us to our knees
just to make it through the night.
Though the universe prefers
that every soul awakens gently,
there are unexpected events in life
that rough us up in the dark.
In times like these,
God comforts us face to face.

Heaven on Earth

The human brain has evolved over millions of years
into a complex neural computer capable of processing
over 400 billion bits of information every second.
However, our brains are not who we ultimately are,
but prisms refracting the light of our consciousness
into matter to manifest the world of our making.
Those focused solely on reaching heaven *after* death
ignore the reality of heaven as a state of mind.
As co-creators with the universe, we have the potential
to create whatever version of heaven we desire *now*
while living on earth.

Between Two Rocks

When life pressures you

beyond your normal limitations,

a breakthrough in consciousness

can't be far behind.

When stuck between two rocks,

let the silence speak.

You'll likely hear the reassuring voice

of intuition offer a solution

to your dilemma, or a means of escape.

Surrendering to the silence,

you change the atomic structure

of your present reality

to that of infinite possibilities.

Wedged between two rocks can be painful,

but isn't pain just another way

God communicates?

Prepare for Adventure

When preparing to enter etheric realms,

spiritual guides suggest packing light.

Mystics carry an oak staff representing wisdom,

a finely-cut emerald for third-eye clarity,

and a pendant symbolizing their inner quest.

Those who've explored spiritual realms say:

square away your life beforehand—

pare your possessions, strengthen your belief,

and resolve any unfinished business

you might have with others, even if they've passed on.

As with any journey exploring the unknown,

stay disciplined, focused, and optimistic.

And if you come across a junction in the road,

always choose the road with the best views.

Take the Leap

Leaping into the void

from the comfort of your life

is like skydiving for the first time.

Though you've been reassured

a thousand times your parachute

will open smoothly and you'll touch

the ground below in one piece,

fear of the unknown

keeps most clinging

to the frame of the exit door.

But once you overcome your fear

and take the leap,

you'll finally feel the full

exhilaration of your life.

The Eternal Moment

A breakthrough in consciousness
is like the moment a shipwrecked sailor,
having lost all hope of being rescued,
finally sights land.
Or the artist searching for his muse,
catching his or her glance
from across a crowded ferry.
In that transcendent moment
the veil between worlds lifts,
and the entire orchestra of heaven
breaks free from the clouds.

A Lively Destination

The world of spirit is not an endless stretch of nothingness

devoid of colorful characters,

inspired architecture, or palatial gardens.

Quite the opposite.

Those who've accessed causal realms,

from lower astral planes to the higher dimensions,

describe the world of spirit as a spiraling galaxy of light,

populated by an ever-evolving hierarchy of souls—

your own soul included.

Because the underdeveloped neurotransmitters of our brains

barely register higher frequencies of matter,

most imagine spirit to be as barren as the moon.

But to the mystic's eye, the world of spirit

is just as lively as any place found on earth.

The Hero's Quest

For greater insight

into who you are as a spiritual being,

why not embrace the classic role of the hero

who embarks on an epic journey

in search of life's deeper meaning?

You need only weigh anchor and set sail

to where your soul yearns to be free.

But prepare for a lifelong odyssey.

Opening the portals to inner knowledge,

there's no turning back.

And though you needn't give up everything

to know yourself as a spiritual being,

those who've sailed to distant shores

say it often helps.

Causal Realms

Think back to when you hiked

deep into the rugged mountains

to leave the world behind

and commune with nature.

Didn't those treks into the wilderness

clear your head and lift your spirits?

Likely those heightened experiences

still resonate in your memory today.

Why not explore new destinations,

some even more revitalizing?

Have you ever questioned whether

time, God, or heaven exists?

Or where your soul travels to in dreams

or after death?

With pen and journal,

having entered a meditative state,

why not explore the dreamscapes

of your higher mind?

Heaven Opens

Severing family ties, moving cross-country,

searching the world over—

just to glimpse the light of eternity.

Having reached the water's edge,

the secret to life arrives on a wing.

Countless years begging God for answers,

heaven finally responds.

Above a twilight sea the sky catches fire.

An orange glow bursts across the horizon,

spreading its reflection on the water below.

A lifetime of longing breaks free.

Then an angel appears,

and the secret to life is revealed

in the beauty of a sunset.

Message of the Immortals

Just as Beethoven, Galileo, and the Buddha

rocked the world in their lifetimes,

you have the same potential to do so in your life.

Because every soul is evolving in consciousness,

you were born to discover cures, break records,

and help usher in a more enlightened age.

By living an inspired life, you fortify the antahkarana of light—

the spiritual bridge that connects souls on earth

to the knowledge and wisdom of the higher dimensions.

And what advice do the immortals offer the world?

Be conscious in every moment;

know yourself as a spiritual being;

and whatever your dreams, reach for the stars.

The Higher Dimensions

Those who've opened their minds to the higher dimensions

say there's more to life than what most believe.

Having explored spiritual realms strengthened their faith,

heightened their intuition, and lessened their fear of death.

Mystics contend that one needn't die first to enter heaven.

In meditation, Rishis have detailed healing retreats,

Akashic libraries, and temples housing vortices of energy

that give souls easier transport between dimensions.

Those having had near-death experiences recount

embracing loved ones and having visions of the future.

With the dawning of a more enlightened age,

spiritual beings tending the portals between worlds predict

an influx of souls on earth visiting the 4th and 5th dimensions.

To begin, open your mind to the possibility

there's more to life than what you presently believe.

Chapter 6

Your Purpose on Earth

130   There's More to Life

133   Your Higher Calling

135   Your Promise

136   Discovering Your Purpose

139   Life Isn't a Race

140   What Counts for More

142   Wisdom's Light

144   Make Believe Again

146   Heed the Call

148   Living Fully

151   Angels in Embodiment

153   Unfinished Business

There's More to Life

Many have this nagging sense

that something is missing in their lives.

They feel lost and disillusioned,

that life is passing them by.

Nothing seems to fill the void.

Some begin to question the meaning of life:

What's my purpose? Does God exist?

Will I ever experience true happiness?

Seeking answers, they embark

on a mystical journey, questioning

their inner motives, who they're with,

where they live, what the future holds.

Some begin quietly, observing

the path that rivers take to the sea;

how one kind act can change a life;

or how, by living in the present moment,

God speaks to them directly.

Your Higher Calling

Do you have an overriding passion or calling in life
that catapults you out of bed every morning?
Is your dream to change the world for the better—
heal the sick, run for office, or save the planet?
At a soul level, everyone aspires to accomplish
something meaningful in their lives.
If your calling is to broker peace, build bridges,
or express yourself through the arts,
given the strength of your constancy and desire,
the universe provides every opportunity
for you to succeed, and all you must do in return
is surrender to a higher power how it all unfolds.
Only then can the universe work unencumbered
to pull together all the details of your dream.

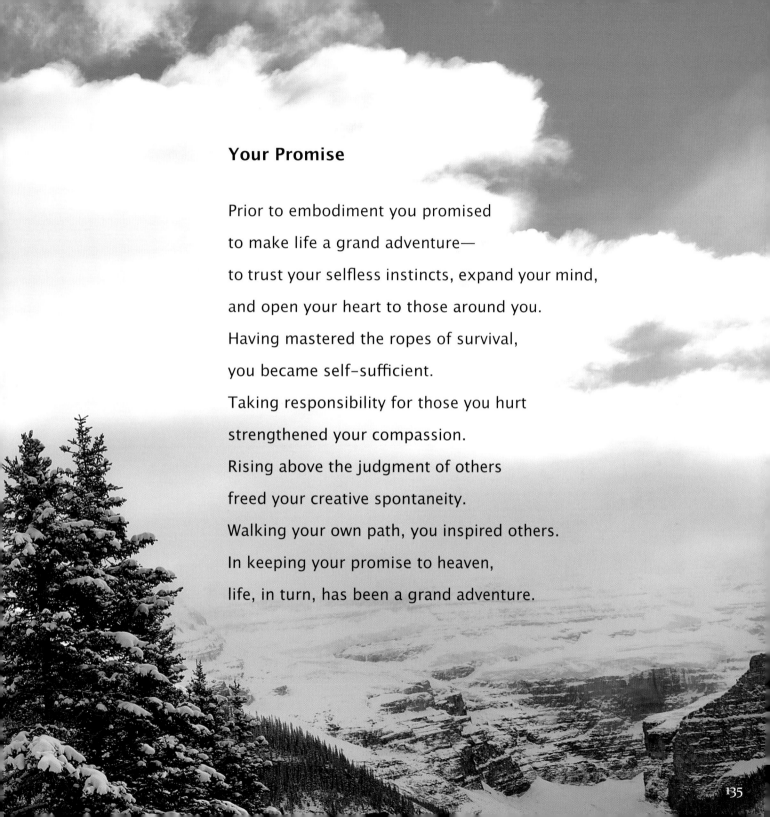

Your Promise

Prior to embodiment you promised

to make life a grand adventure—

to trust your selfless instincts, expand your mind,

and open your heart to those around you.

Having mastered the ropes of survival,

you became self-sufficient.

Taking responsibility for those you hurt

strengthened your compassion.

Rising above the judgment of others

freed your creative spontaneity.

Walking your own path, you inspired others.

In keeping your promise to heaven,

life, in turn, has been a grand adventure.

Discovering Your Purpose

Those who say life has little or no purpose

are like shipwrecked sailors hopelessly

marooned on tiny, uncharted islands.

Though many discover their purpose early in life,

others must sail across the dark void

to the furthest regions of their imaginations

while fending off the sirens of apathy

intent on veering their ship into the rocks.

But those who've sailed to distant shores

say the journey itself is life's purpose,

and that by charting their own course,

and overcoming their fear of the unknown,

adventure is theirs for the sailing.

Life Isn't a Race

True success is an inner quest,

the highest measure being:

How many in your life did you love,

inspire, and comfort?

Comparing yourself to those

seemingly ahead in the world

restricts your soul to the treadmill

of endless competition.

There will always be someone

coming up from behind to overtake you.

Success by comparison is a losing game.

The goal of life isn't a frantic race

up a mountain to plant a flag.

It's offering your hand to those below

who have fallen behind.

What Counts for More

Having traveled far and wide

along unfamiliar roads,

the obstacles you overcame

define the person you've become.

Wisdom gained instilled

a deeper love for others.

Self-reflection brought

greater clarity of heart and mind.

And though you let yourself

and others down at times,

you took responsibility.

Fame and fortune may have eluded you,

but on your final breath,

those you loved count for more.

Wisdom's Light

Some make their struggles excuses

to complain, blame, or withdraw,

while others see them as opportunities

to exercise their abilities and creativity.

Every struggle contains the light of wisdom.

When released, it halos your character

and defines your capacity to overcome

life's challenges down the road.

By overcoming your personal struggles,

you increase hope and inspiration

for those who follow in your footsteps.

Having overcome *their* struggles,

artists, explorers, and mystics created

masterworks of art, opened new frontiers,

and widened the pathways of love

to flow directly between our hearts.

Make Believe Again

Those who build castles from sand

do so, first, by believing they can.

Before entering the arena of dreams,

believe yourself to be immortal.

Run with wolves, sail uncharted seas,

paraglide above the Great Pyramid.

Look deeply in the mirror.

Is your image that of the dreamer

you aspire to be? If not, why not?

Real dreamers, like wizards,

change reality by the flick of their wands.

Remember when you pretended

to fly jets, or cup the stars in your hands?

Why not create the same magic today

as you did believing as a child?

Heed the Call

Artists, poets, musicians—you are summoned!

Heed the call for an enlightened age to be defined,

not by greed or conflict, hate and war,

but by love, understanding, and respect for all.

You are summoned to scour realms of myth and legend

for golden fleeces and holy grails.

Visionaries! Help bridge the human divide.

Disarm nations, inspire hope, find common ground.

In eternal realms, the answers to humanity's

seemingly impossible challenges can be found.

Brazen souls! Storm heaven's gates and snatch

the blueprints for a saner, brighter future.

Those who've reconciled their need for power,

fame, and fortune—awaken to your higher purpose!

Artists in every creative field: Inspire humanity

to break the shackles of fear, and live life fully.

Living Fully

Living fully demands an inquisitive mind,
an empathetic heart, a sharp accountant,
and a stationary bike to let off steam.
Living fully is a full-time job.
While many chug along in life without conviction,
others strive single-mindedly to create a better world,
forgoing bigger paychecks to pursue a dream
of exploring the ocean in a submarine,
living with gorillas in the Congo,
building schools for girls in Mozambique,
or, like Vincent Van Gogh,
painting the "marvelous light"
in the South of France.
Living fully isn't always easy,
and may not pay the bills,
but that's the price you pay
for happiness.

Angels in Embodiment

Millions across the planet awaken each morning

determined to make a difference in the world.

Through self-reflection, meditation,

living balanced lives, and serving the needs of others,

they act as spiritual counterpoints to those

who foment hate and division on the planet.

Foster parents, social workers, environmentalists,

activists, therapists—all serving the greater good.

Some would even dive into an icy lake

or storm a burning building to save a stranger.

Because everyone is struggling with something in life,

these embodied angels look for every opportunity

to give an extra dose of love to everyone they meet.

Unfinished Business

To know your purpose in life,

recall those times you came close to death.

Times when an angel appeared

and plucked you from the bony clutches

of your worst nightmare

and set you down on firmer ground.

What divine hand pulled you back from the brink?

Or, when you fell asleep at the wheel,

awakened you just in time

before you would have crashed and died.

There are no accidents in the universe.

You were saved for a good reason.

Somewhere in your past you earned a second chance.

Your life was extended because

someone, or the world, still needs you.

Chapter 7

Change the World

156   Embrace Change

159   Planetary Survival

161   You Can Too

162   The Mirror of Others

165   By Their Bold Strokes

167   Trust the Universe

169   Hope for Humanity

170   Budding Alchemists

173   Truth Be Known

175   Wisdom of Nature

176   Laid Bare

178   Why?

180   Diplomats of Peace

183   Evolutionary Leap

Embrace Change

It's only a matter of time before any of us

experiences a major loss in life.

To offset the pain or suffering, the sage embraces

every form of change in his life beforehand.

Not to say that the death of a loved one

or a chronic illness wouldn't test him—*it would.*

Spiritual masters are not immune to having

their hearts torn in two or feeling great loss.

The sage prepares for such eventualities

by strengthening his joy and optimism,

cultivating deeper relationships, and keeping

the illusions of the world in perspective.

So when the time comes, and the swells

of his emotions attempt to overwhelm him,

he can draw on his spiritual practices

and lean on close friends to see him through.

Planetary Survival

To help reverse the damage done to the planet,

we must resolve to live in greater harmony

with ourselves, each other, and our environment.

Man's insatiable need to always triumph over nature

has brought us to a level of human unsustainability.

Though we've expanded our depth of knowledge

through the internet, developed miracle cures,

set foot on the moon, and created sublime architecture,

if the planet is to come back into balance,

we must change our thinking and destructive ways.

As earth nears a tipping point in its survival,

there's no time to waste with our heads in the sand.

You Can Too

So many in a hurry, yet are they any happier
once they arrive? So many working jobs
or living in homes or cities they find uninspiring.
So many have everything, yet feel empty inside.
Then there are those who barely catch their breath
giving their time or what they have to others.
Those who invent things to make living easier,
those who work tirelessly for peace and justice,
those who treat the sick, and those who work
without rest to raise well-balanced children.
And don't forget healers, protectors, teachers,
and those who inspire others to carry on.
Or nations defending nations from aggressors,
or assisting them in the wake of disasters.
Each day, millions leave their comfortable homes
to make a difference in the world.

The Mirror of Others

Everyone in life is either your teacher or student—

oftentimes both.

We attract family, friends, and acquaintances

to help awaken us to our higher purpose.

The sage listens attentively to those around him

to glean the inspiration and wisdom each imparts.

As everyone is essential to the whole and harmony of humanity,

when being kind to others, and forgiving those

who've harmed us in any way, we lighten our burden.

To know if you're holding up your end

of life's spiritual bargain, observe those around you.

Everyone orbiting your life is either a positive

or negative reflection of your consciousness.

Each is a reminder of the progress you've made, or not,

to free yourself from life's karmic wheel.

By Their Bold Strokes

Throughout history,
creative individuals
turned the known world
upside down for the better.
By their bold strokes,
they painted a brighter future
on the ever-changing canvas
of human evolution.
Driven by their passion,
visionaries in every field
stood resolute before
the naysayers of their time.
And what did they hope
to achieve by their work?
Only to offer the world
a grander portrait of itself.

Trust the Universe

If your passion in life is to make the world
a better place, patrons in every field
are waiting in the wings to assist you.
If your music, film, book, art, or invention
gives hope to the world, or to a single person,
you'll attract the benefactors needed
to sponsor your worthwhile service or creation.
By assisting you, they advance in the ranks
of esteemed men and women.
If you've honed your skills and talents,
and your offering inspires the dreams of others,
the universe is compelled by its very existence
to bring to your doorstep those willing
to help advance your worthy dream.

Hope for Humanity

More fear, ignorance, and superstition

revolves around higher spiritual truth

than every conspiracy theory concocted on earth.

Consequently, few have consciously applied cosmic law

to fulfill their personal needs and dreams.

Fewer yet have tapped the wisdom and treasures

awaiting them in the higher dimensions.

Because most religions reject progressive revelation,

relying instead on scripture penned eons ago,

seekers of truth wander aimlessly through life.

Yet, despite the shortcomings of our age,

humanity must be doing something right.

How do explain so many loving relationships

flourishing in the world?

Budding Alchemists

Across the cultural spectrum,

the natural role of every parent is to love,

support, and guide their offspring.

In turn, children are expected to show

respect for their caregivers, perform

basic household chores, and express

gratitude for what they've been given.

But those parents who teach their children

higher cosmic law serve them longer.

Leaving home, these budding alchemists

intuitively know when and how

to apply such wisdom to attract their needs.

Those who learned their lessons well

are rarely found wanting.

Truth Be Known

Scientific breakthroughs have improved our lives.

We no longer communicate by drums,

hunker in caves, or travel by stagecoach.

We now reside in solar-powered homes,

and crisscross the planet in supersonic jets.

Computers and high-speed internet

give us access to virtually unlimited knowledge.

But when it comes to understanding

the mysteries of spirit, most remain clueless.

Some still believe a bearded deity

rules heaven and earth, that we only have

one lifetime to reach our full potential,

or that our souls cease to exist after death.

As man evolves, such ideas will fade into oblivion

like the flat earth theory,

or the geocentric belief that our planet

resides at the center of the universe.

Wisdom of Nature

Cosmic order is on full display when viewing nature's starry constellations.

Thunder rumbling through her forests alerts her creatures of a coming storm.

Her subtle color palette comes alive after spring rains awaken mountain meadows.

Decaying autumn leaves invigorate the soil every living being relies upon.

In the stillness of the night you can hear the celestial humming of her spheres.

Ocean shells pressed against our ears relay a timeless message to our souls.

Wisdom can be gleaned by observing how she gets along with herself and others.

So when nature says the planet is in peril, shouldn't we pay more attention?

Laid Bare

Our souls are reflected in the seasons,

and none more starkly than in winter.

No other time of the year can you hear

the whirling of creation so audibly.

As days grow shorter and food scarcer,

winter can test the heartiest of souls.

Those unprepared for the long stretches

of gray skies can easily lose their way.

To make it through the cold nights,

many cope by drawing closer to the hearth,

gripping the hands of angels tighter,

and driving their faith harder.

But having laid bare with God in winter

strengthens our souls to break free

from the hard ground in spring,

and flow wildly like summer's sweet nectar.

Why?

Why are poverty, racism, and tribal hatred
still rampant in our civilized world?
Why in the name of God do religious fanatics
continue to oppress and murder those
of different races, nationalities, beliefs,
or cultures that tolerate freer lifestyles?
Why are so many religions bent on conversion
rather than promoting diversity?
What isn't being advocated in churches,
mosques, temples, schools, or town squares
to inoculate humanity against these
debilitating diseases of the heart and mind?
Moreover, why aren't the same resources
that militarize our planet being channeled
into peace, love, and cooperation between
nations, religions, and individuals?

Diplomats of Peace

Diplomats of peace strategically position themselves
throughout the world where they're needed most—
spiritual ambassadors tasked with the responsibility
of lessening the karmic burdens of humanity.
Mindful of their influence over family, friends,
and strangers, wise, old souls conduct the flow of love,
hope, and understanding between us.
Conscious of their transforming role in society,
they look for every opportunity to acknowledge
the redeeming qualities inherent in everyone.
Because each of us possesses a degree of wisdom,
when diplomats of peace listen intently to others,
something profound in themselves is revealed.

Evolutionary Leap

Since the Age of Enlightenment,

the thrust of mankind has been focused

on unraveling the mysteries of the cosmos.

In every field, scientists are attempting

to prove what the mystics say is true.

Even God's existence is being put to the test

with particle-beam accelerators.

The thinking is, if man can prove God exists,

in whatever form, truth is the beneficiary.

Yet some cry foul: Truth relies on faith,

and the old prophets have the final word.

But what is faith? Don't science and religion

spring from the same omnipresent source?

Only by honoring the truth in both

can humanity take the next evolutionary step

toward greater oneness with all.

Chapter 8

Be Nothing

186   Let No One Define You

189   Be Yourself Today

191   The Ultimate Quest

192   Be Free to Fly

194   Your Teacher and Guide

196   The Way of Nature

199   Staying Optimistic

201   Eternal Realms

Let No One Define You

Be no one in this moment—

neither husband, wife, or favorite daughter.

Sever your ties to the competitive world.

Open the shutters of your mind.

Be as light as moonlit snow.

Shake off others' expectations.

You no longer need to chase happiness,

friendships, love, money, or redemption—

let them chase you for a change.

In the peacefulness of knowing

you're loved for being you,

you needn't please anyone any longer—

not even God.

Be Yourself Today

Crumple your list of things to do

and claim this day your own.

Take the next exit, park your mind,

and relax your shoulders.

Say, *I've had enough* to whoever

or whatever holds you hostage.

You needn't be anywhere

but where you are in this moment.

Let the lightness of your being

draw you high above a tranquil lake.

Observe the cool morning mist

gently greet the light of dawn.

Watch a mother osprey glide to her nest

to feed her hungry chicks.

Life is more than lists of things to do.

Awaken! Join nature's chorus.

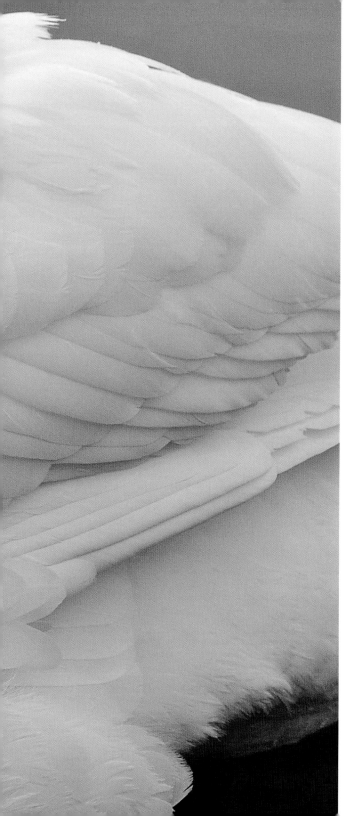

The Ultimate Quest

Within the creative parameters

governing cosmic law

you have free will to be anyone

and do anything you desire.

The mystic pursues freedom of his soul

that he might overcome the constraints

of time, place, and gravity.

He harnesses the power of his mind

and summons his will to soar

high above the illusions of the world.

And because his love of others

gives his spirit flight,

every person he encounters

is an opportunity for him to fly.

Be Free to Fly

Flying *is* possible.

Haven't you flown above trees in dreams?

To gain lift, let go of always having to be

in charge of everything and everyone.

Remember a time in your past

when you had a major breakthrough—

perhaps as a toddler about to take your first steps?

Didn't the anticipation of running free

propel your feet and arms forward?

Flying above life is no different.

Let go of all that keeps you earthbound.

In the space of nothingness,

beyond judgment, envy, worry, or regret,

outside all known laws of physics,

the runway of life is clear for takeoff.

Your Teacher and Guide

The universe is your teacher and guide,

fully aware of you as a uniquely evolving soul.

Unlike the mindless echo chamber

many believe it to be, the universe possesses

an infinite degree of anticipatory awareness

of everything your soul requires.

Like an astute teacher

who provides a struggling student

with an extra boost of encouragement,

or a conscientious mother

escorting her children across a busy street,

the all-intelligent universe,

like any devoted teacher or parent,

inspires and guides us throughout our lives.

The Way of Nature

As the North Pole tilts closer to the sun,

the frozen landscape of winter gives way

to lilac-scented breezes, warm rains,

and an overnight explosion of growth.

What better time of the year than spring

to observe the beauty, economy,

and creativity of nature, when the elements of earth

work seamlessly together?

Likely, you've already mastered

many of nature's lessons to satisfy your needs.

Hasn't taking the path of least resistance,

bending your branches in the wind,

or living in harmony with the natural world

given you easier access to nature's

greenest valleys, her most dramatic sunsets,

and brightest stars?

Staying Optimistic

Nature always finds a way

to stay in balance with herself.

If you can navigate a forest like the wind,

find the quickest route to the sea like a river,

or grow a flower in the crack of a sidewalk,

you've mastered three of nature's

more amazing feats.

When in harmony with the rhythms

of the natural world,

you will always gravitate

to the perfect time and place

where your soul is favored to evolve.

Focusing on what works in life

rather than what doesn't,

you begin to understand how nature

remains so optimistic.

Eternal Realms

Drawing closer to the realms

of eternal nothingness,

aspens along a rocky ridge

break out in polite applause.

As the cool night air blankets

the final flickers of day,

a great horned owl swoops down

from her sturdy perch.

As the forest offers up its secrets,

the Grand Rotunda—

that etheric hall of wisdom—

rises on the horizon, translucent.

Entering its marble halls,

answers to life's questions

swirl around your head

like lotus petals on a breeze.

Chapter 9

Be a Dreamer

205   Be a Dreamer

206   Bare Your Soul

208   For Dreams to Grow

211   Unfold Your Maps

213   Birthing Dreams

215   Life's Richest Souls

217   Where Dreams Begin

219   Reflections

221   Seafaring Dreamers

222   Advice to Dreamers

225   The Sage's Way

Be a Dreamer

The highest honor the world bestows on anyone

is that of the practical dreamer.

So why waste time working a mediocre job

or amassing a fortune you'll never spend?

Why not be a dreamer like Jackie Robinson,

Jonas Salk, Greta Thunberg, or Walt Disney?

As everyone delights seeing children play,

why not lose yourself in dreams?

Be the baseball player, scientist, activist,

or film producer, you were born to be.

Practical dreamers are those who make

the most of scaling their imaginations.

Yet, some believe dreaming is a waste of time,

that fate always has the upper hand.

But what of those who made a better world

having lived their wildest dreams?

Bare Your Soul

To live your dreams

stand on stage and bare your soul.

What!? *Bare my soul!?*

Yes!

Who said doing anything worthwhile was easy?

Not God.

God's only promise:

The higher you climb, the better the views.

If you need inspiration, as everyone does,

seek out those living their dreams.

Ask if they're fulfilled, and if they are,

they'll likely confide that nothing compares

to saddling up each morning

and riding out to touch the edges of the sun.

And if they're living their dreams for all the right reasons,

they'll turn and say:

If your dream inspires the dreams of others,

consider your life a success.

For Dreams to Grow

If you haven't amassed a small fortune

or walked on water yet, there's work ahead.

You were born to break free of the earth,

open your petals, and bask in the sun.

Every dream demands a gardener's touch:

tilling, seeding, watering, and weeding.

Dreams give pleasure and purpose to life.

To grow, you must grow alongside them.

Unfold Your Maps

Pack your bags, untether your life,

and cast off to where the winds

of the adventurer press against your face.

Live along the sea in a small Italian village.

Kayak up the crystal rivers

that etch the rugged landscape of Montana.

Scramble up the Andes

and feel the ancient magic of Machu Picchu.

Live as if anything is possible.

There's no better time to unfold your maps

and chart a course to destinations

beyond the limitations

of what others say is practical.

You have an obligation to your eternal soul

to live as if nothing holds you back.

Birthing Dreams

Despite your present circumstances,

you have the same potential as anyone

to birth your dreams and live them colorfully.

What greater purpose in life?

Dreams define your soul made manifest.

But dreams need birthing—

which, for some, can be difficult.

You must overcome your doubts and fears,

and boldly navigate around or through

whatever keeps them from breaking free.

Birthing dreams isn't always easy,

but unless you try, nothing comes of life.

Life's Richest Souls

When living the full expression of your dreams,

your heart, mind, and spirit resonate as one.

If acting on Broadway, landing on the moon,

or painting *plein air* landscapes inspires you,

until you apply that first stroke of paint on the canvas,

you'll never know what you're capable of.

What's more exhilarating than taking the stage,

rocketing into space, or creating art

surrounded by nature's palette of light?

Whatever you do that expresses your spirit

attracts the eye of the goddess of good fortune.

Yet some say dreaming is impractical—

that you'll never make a decent living.

In reality, the universe is exceptionally generous

to those who pursue their wildest dreams.

Those doing what they love most are,

by every measure, life's richest souls.

Where Dreams Begin

To know yourself
is to know your dreams.
Living another's dream
assumes their shadow.
If feeling lost, unworthy,
or misunderstood, clear out
the cobwebbed furniture
stored in your attic.
Let go of those causing you
endless grief and pain.
Face the afternoon sun
and shout out everything
you've been holding back.
To know your dreams
is to know yourself.

Reflections

There's a point in your life when you must stop looking.

No one but you knows the secret to your happiness.

Decide now to live your best life, and stick to it.

There are those who love you in both good and bad times.

They are your trusty companions. Hold them close.

Keep your library of inspirational books at eye level.

Pull one out each night and read a page or two at bedtime.

Commit to follow your higher, humble instincts.

Monitor what goes into and comes out of your mouth.

Pay attention to your thoughts; take a deep breath when

your accounts sink below water, friends disappoint you,

or the country fails to meet your sane expectations.

Take control of what you can, let go of what you can't.

Give your dreams plenty of runway to take off and land.

Yes, you'll fail at times, forgetting your promise.

It's not the end of the world. Just get back in the saddle.

Seafaring Dreamers

There are those who sail for lifetimes

in search of the eternal flame.

They claim the sun, moon, stars,

and every new horizon as their own.

They'll only captain ships that sail

for treasure and adventure.

They'll navigate uncharted seas

to prove that God exists, or not.

They'll confront every monster known,

and risk everything they own

just to touch the cloak of immortality.

Seafaring dreamers are the heroes

that animate our timeless myths,

for they believe that dreaming

is the wind that billows our sails.

Advice to Dreamers

Embrace the heart, mind, and spirit

of the dreamer you're destined to become.

Consult the experts in every field of life.

Bend convention to advance your selfless goals.

Push back when critics say your dream

is too impractical—*what do they know*?

If your dream advances peace in the world,

join those already in the trenches.

If your dream inspires others to live theirs,

success in life is guaranteed.

If your dream is bigger than yourself,

wear the cloak of humility.

But if your dream is to love and be loved,

prepare to give up everything.

The Sage's Way

From the sage's point of view, there are two basic guidelines to life:

Be mindful in every moment, and embrace the light in everyone.

What greater wisdom? It's the path every enlightened being walks.

Love and mindfulness open the doors to higher consciousness.

When loving others without judgment or expectations, like the sage,

you'll fly high above the drama and illusions of the world.

And isn't flying on your list of things to master in life? It is for sages.

Photos

Chapter 1

Pgs. 2-3 Cottonwood Lake in the Crazy Mountains, Montana
Pgs. 4-5 Jo; Antibes, France
Pgs. 6-7 Charlene and Napa along the Yellowstone river; Livingston, Montana
Pg. 8 One-month-old Timber wolf pups, Raven and Shilo; Howlers Inn and Wolf Sanctuary outside Bozeman, Montana
Pgs. 10-11 The cold waters of Lake Michigan; Sleeping Bear Dunes National Park near Traverse City, Michigan
Pgs. 12-13 Swans on DePuy Pond; Paradise Valley, Montana
Pgs. 14-15 Sunset on the Ligurian Sea; Manarola, Italy
Pgs. 16-17 Sandhill crane; Paradise Valley, Montana
Pgs. 18-19 Connecticut woods in autumn
Pgs. 20-21 Mourning Cloak butterfly on lilac; Livingson, Montana
Pgs. 22-23 Trailhead rain puddle; Crazy Mountains, Montana
Pgs. 24-25 Woman climbing a boulder; Lamar Valley, Yellowstone National Park

Chapter 2

Pgs. 28-29 Charlene posing alongside "Untitled (to Francis)" metal sculpture by Antony Gormley at the Tate Modern Museum; London, England
Pgs. 30-31 Charlene overlooking mountain lake in southwest Montana
Pg. 32 Andrew and Anne-Gaelle under a covered bridge; Vallarta Botanical Gardens; Puerto Vallarta, Mexico
Pgs. 34-35 Older couple holding hands; Cote d'Azur, France

Pgs. 36-37 Anne-Gaelle at the Vallarta Botanical Gardens; Puerto Vallarta, Mexico
Pgs. 38-39 Place de Gaulle fountains erupting; Antibes, France
Pgs. 40-41 Great Egret foraging for food off Masons Island, Connecticut
Pg. 42 A mat of Alpine forget-me-nots (Myosotis asiatica) atop a mountain in southwest Montana
Pg. 44 Mackenzie creating large bubbles on Main street; Bozeman, Montana

Chapter 3

Pgs. 48-49 Thai exchange student, Joy, experiencing autumn leaves for the first time; Livingston, Montana
Pgs. 50-51 Stone walkway at Vallarta Botanical Gardens; Puerto Vallarta, Mexico
Pgs. 52-53 Leigh Lake shoreline; Grand Teton National Park, Wyoming
Pgs. 54-55 Nathaniel fly fishing on Emerald Lake; Hyalite Canyon, Montana
Pg. 57-58 Colin; Niantic, Connecticut
Pgs. 58-59 Mother and daughters along the River Thames Path; London, England
Pgs. 60-61 Titan Sunflower with bee; Livingston, Montana
Pgs. 62-63 The Old Town of Antibes on the Mediterranean Sea; Antibes, France
Pg. 64 Stone Mason building a wall near the Picasso Museum; Antibes, France
Pgs. 66-67 Charlene meditating on a double rainbow across the Yellowstone River; Livingston, Montana
Pgs. 68-69 Skateboarder on a July 4th parade float; Livingston, Montana
Pgs. 70-71 Mansion on DePuy Pond; Paradise Valley, Montana

Chapter 4

Pgs. 74-75 Hiking the Elephant Head Trail; Absaroka-Beartooth Mountains, Montana
Pg. 76 Young couple holding hands after a yoga class; Antibes, France
Pgs. 78-79 Mackenzie contemplating her future while visiting her grandfather in Livingston, Montana
Pgs. 80-81 Unplucked roses clutched in woman's hands; Florence, Italy
Pgs. 82-83 Hollowed out gourd filled with natural found objects
Pgs. 84-85 Fly fisherman on the Yellowstone River; Yellowstone National Park
Pgs. 86-87 Leigh Lake stones; Grand Teton National Park, Wyoming
Pgs. 88-89 Hiker contemplating the beauty of Yellowstone National Park
Pgs. 90-91 Two small stones on the shore of Leigh Lake; Grand Teton National Park
Pgs. 92-93 Wetland grasses; Montana
Pgs. 94-95 Dancer Pose; Lamar Valley; Yellowstone National Park, Wyoming
Pgs. 96-97 Park visitor drinking in the beauty of Yellowstone National Park; Montana

Chapter 5

Pgs. 100-101 Boulder River Meadows hiker; Absaroka Range, Montana
Pgs. 102-103 Absaroka mountains in early fall; Paradise Valley, Montana
Pgs. 104-105 Nathaniel and Aurelie at the September 11 Memorial; New York City
Pgs. 106-107 Ocean beach in the remote fishing village of Yelapa, Mexico
Pgs. 108-109 Three rocks on the shoreline of Leigh Lake, Grand Teton National Park

Pgs. 110-111 Hiking in winter to Grotto Falls; Hyalite Canyon, Montana

Pgs. 112-113 Leaping from a boulder into the Ligurian Sea; Manarola, Italy

Pgs. 114-115 Late afternoon light on the Absaroka-Beartooth Mountains; Paradise Valley, Montana

Pgs. 116-117 Sculpture garden in a medieval hilltop town in southern France

Pgs. 118-119 Sailboats on the Mediterranean Sea; Antibes, France

Pgs. 120-121 Hiking around Jenny Lake; Grand Teton National Park, Wyoming

Pgs. 122-123 Sunset on the Mediterranean sea; Antibes, France

Pgs. 124-125 Ruins of a castle; Provence, France

Pgs. 126-127 The Phoenix, an off-grid home in the Greater World Earthship Community near Tres Piedras, New Mexico

Chapter 6

Pgs. 130-131 Backpackers on the Rosebud Trail near Cooke City, Montana

Pgs. 132-133 Standing on Elephant Head mountain; Absaroka Range, Montana

Pgs. 134-135 Mountain peak surrounding Lake Louise in the Banff National Park; Alberta, Canada

Pgs. 136-137 Section of driftwood on Leigh Lake shore; Grand Teton National Park

Pgs. 138-139 Charlene resting by a stream; Elephanthead Mountain, Montana

Pgs. 140-141 Field along the Yellowstone River south of Livingston, Montana

Pgs. 142-143 Backpackers pausing near thermal features while hiking around Shoshone Lake; Yellowstone National Park

Pgs. 144-145 Boys crossing stream; Devil's Hopyard State Park, Connecticut

Pg. 147 Sketch artists on the steps of a hill overlooking Florence, Italy

Pgs. 148-149 Street musician playing his cello under a bridge; London, England

Pg. 150 Bride and her ring bearer outside Antibes Town Hall; Antibes, France

Pgs. 152-153 Sleeping Bear Dunes National Park above Lake Michigan near Traverse City, Michigan

Chapter 7

Pgs. 156-157 Fallen autumn oak leaves on Masons Island, Connectitut

Pgs. 158-159 Great Blue Heron on a branch overlooking Paradise Valley, Montana

Pgs. 160-161 Charlene in a meadow of wildflowers alongside Trout Lake; Yellowstone National Park; Wyoming

Pg. 163 Tourist family on the River Thames Path; London, England

Pgs. 164-165 Artist painting piano keys for a TV commercial; London, England

Pgs. 166-167 Charlene on the Rosebud Trail near Cooke City, Montana

Pgs. 168-169 Deer along a ridge; Paradise Valley, Montana

Pgs. 170-171 Grandfather and granddaughter at a public fountain; Florence, Italy

Pgs. 172-173 The Nomade, sculpture by Juame Plensa; Antibes, France

Pgs. 174-175 Winter storm in Paradise Valley, Montana

Pgs. 176-177 Paradise Valley in winter with deer south of Livingston, Montana

Pgs. 178-179 Jupiter et Encelade by Anne & Patrick Poirier; outdoor sculpture at the Picasso Museum; Antibes, France

Pgs. 180-181 Provincial Market cobblestones; Antibes, France

Pgs. 182-183 Ancient village drinking fountain; Alpes-Maritimes, France

Chapter 8

Pgs. 186-187 Boys at Pine Creek Lake; Absaroka-Beartooth Mountains, Montana

Pgs. 188-189 Small lake south of Livingston; Paradise Valley, Montana

Pgs. 190-191 Preening Trumpeter swan on Fleshman Creek; Livingston, Montana

Pgs. 192-193 Father guiding his daughter along the shank of an old sailing ship's anchor; London, England

Pgs. 194-195 Father and son bonding on a park bench along the Yellowstone River; Livingston, Montana

Pgs. 196-197 Sunset above the Ligurian Sea off the eastern coast of Italy

Pgs. 198-199 Pocket-size waterfall; Crazy Mountains, Montana

Pgs. 200-201 Boulder River, Montana

Chapter 9

Pgs. 204-205 Fawn peering out of the tall grass; Livingston, Montana

Pgs. 206-207 Street singer along the River Thames; London, England

Pgs. 208-209 Elandssuurvy flowers (carpobrotus Acinaciformis) along the Mediterranean; Cap d'Antibes, France

Pgs. 210-211 Seaside fishing village of Manarola in the province of La Spezia in northwest Italy

Pgs. 212-213 The look of wonder. Mackenzie peering out a window at the Old Tinsley House; Bozeman, Montana

Pg. 214 Actors promoting Disney's Newsies during Livingston's annual Roundup parade (performed in 2019 at the Shane Center for the Arts); Livingston, Montana

Pgs. 216-217 Charlene looking out over a mountain lake; southwest Montana

Pgs. 218-219 Late afternoon light on Mason's Lake; Mason's Island, Connecticut

Pgs. 220-221 Schooner on the Mediterranean Sea off the coast of Antibes, France

Pgs. 222-223 Lily pads; Vallarta Botanical Gardens; Puerto Vallarta, Mexico

Pgs. 224-225 Andrew and Zeus along the Rosebud Trail near Cooke City, Montana

ACKNOWLEDGMENTS Big thanks to Bonnie Murphy, Michelle Bernard, Cynthia Logan, Susan Harrow, Elaine Kimbler, and Ramona Launda for your editorial assistance and feedback. Each in your own way brought greater clarity to these writings. To David S. Lewis, who was an early supporter of my writings, from which *Breaking Through the Mist* emerged. To my youngest son, Brendan, who was always willing to help me through the learning curve of the InDesign graphic program used to create this book. To my eldest son, Thomas, illustrator extraordinaire, who turned my old-school mock-up into the InDesign format. To James Bennett, graphic designer, who helped bring the prepress process over the finish line. And to my patient, loving, and supportive wife, Charlene, who has inspired me over the years to follow my dreams.

INFLUENTIAL BOOKS *Christos* by William Kingsland (1949); *Collected Writings* by Manly P. Hall, Vol 3 (1962); *Revelation: The Divine Fire* by Brad Steiger (1973); *A Parenthesis in Eternity* by Joel Goldsmith (1963); *Tao Te Ching: A New Translation & Commentary* by Ralph Alan Dale (2002); *The Gnostic Gospels* by Elaine Pagels (1979); *Life After Death* by Deepak Chopra (2006); *Wisdom of the Taoists* by Howard Smith (1980); *Creating Miracles* by Carolyn Miller (1995); *The Creative Mind* by Margaret Boden (1990); *In Search of the Miraculous* by P. D. Ouspensky (1949); *The Astral Plane* by C. W. Leadbeater (1933); *The 4th Dimension* by Rudy Rucker (1985); *Secret Splendor* by Charles Essert (1973); *Soul Retrieval* by Sandra Ingerman (1991); and *The Path of Light* by Regina Lorr and Robert Crary (1983).

MODEL RELEASES Because I spontaneously photograph people in public places when I travel, this book contains a few images of individuals I did not secure model releases from at the time. If you're absolutely insistent that your image not appear in this limited edition book, I can remove your photograph on the next print run. However, if you decide to give me permission to use your image, please email your consent to: thomasburns333@gmail.com.

USE OF THE TERM GOD Though I use the term God throughout this book, my belief is not the Christian version of God as "...the eternal being who created and preserves all things...is both transcendent (wholly independent of, and removed from, the material universe) and immanent (involved in the world)." My belief is that God is simply the intelligent and absolute force of the universe. Quoting Theosophical Master Kuthumi: "We know there is in our [solar] system no such thing as God, either personal or impersonal. Para Brahma is not a God, but absolute immutable law. The word 'God' was invented to designate the unknown cause of those effects which man has admired or dreaded without understanding them."

TYPEFACE Constantia, the typeface used throughout most of this book, was designed by John Hudson, and commissioned by Microsoft. It is a transitional serif type influenced by Eric Gill's Perpetua design. Development of the typeface began in 2003, and was released in 2006.

THOMAS BURNS was born in Detroit, Michigan, where he lived until he left for New York City to attend the School of Visual Arts in 1966 on scholarship. As a graphic artist, he worked as art director for poster artist Peter Max in the early '70s, and as production artist on Andy Warhol's *Interview* magazine in the mid-'80s. In 1987, he moved with his wife, Charlene, to Livingston, Montana, where they raised a family and he co-published a monthly tabloid magazine for 11 years. Thomas is the author of six chapbooks of poetry: *Souvenirs, Parallels, Wings of Thought, Of Life, Freedom's Son,* and *Unbound.* Presently, he and Charlene own and operate Howlers Inn and Wolf Sanctuary in the Bridger Canyon outside Bozeman, Montana. Journaling, photography, and caring for wolves are his passions.

The author is available for readings

and workshops.

thomasburns333@gmail.com